Colour Nature Library

VENOMOUS ANIMALS

By

ROBERT BURTON M.A.

Designed by
DAVID GIBBON

Produced by
TED SMART

COLOUR LIBRARY BOOKS

Published 1987 by Colour Library Books Ltd,
Guildford, Surrey, England.
© 1987 Colour Library Ltd.
© Illustrations: Bruce Coleman Ltd.
Printed and bound in Barcelona, Spain by Cronion, S.A.
All rights reserved.
ISBN 0 904681 27 0

INTRODUCTION

Animals dangerous to Man have always excited attention. At one time they were a matter of life and death for everyone, and they still are in the less developed parts of the world. In civilised parts the large carnivores have been destroyed and eradication programmes are aimed at biting insects that spread diseases. Temperate countries are spared even this; there are few animals which can be called a hazard to safety. Nevertheless, dangerous animals, and in particular those which deliver a poisonous bite or sting, hold a particular fascination and horror. This is partly based on ignorance. Our ancestors accepted the wildest stories about the dangers of ferocious and poisonous creatures. Exaggerations of the size of the animal and its capacity to cause grievous bodily harm were commonplace and never challenged, so that, even now, there are some strange ideas about the dangers posed by some animals. There are even harmless animals suffering under the stigma of a bad reputation. In parts of Africa the harmless but bizarre chameleon, which eats insects, is feared more than deadly snakes.

Only in recent times has the scientific study of dangerous animals developed. The impetus came in World War II when thousands of European troops found themselves faced by natural as well as human enemies in tropical theatres of war. Shipwrecked sailors and ditched airmen were confronted with similar problems. Dangerous animals had to be identified and avoided, and their attacks needed proper treatment.

Foremost among the animals studied were those whose venom produces effects hardly commensurate with the size and strength of the animal. A feature of many venomous animals is the fear and horror which they inspire. Yet this is nothing to do with their threat to health. People who would happily gather around tigers, polar bears or buffaloes in a zoo enclosure, shun snakes, scorpions or spiders safely hemmed in by plate glass. Even the knowledge that the species of snake, scorpion or spider is absolutely harmless does nothing to dispel the fear. The fear is deep-seated, apparently irrational, and has been the subject of speculation by psychologists. By compiling careful clinical observations of the victims of venomous animals, researchers have been able to strip away much of the fear, fable, misconception and prejudice surrounding the subject. They have tabulated statistics to find out just how dangerous are venomous animals; they have watched the symptoms of bites and stings and they have compared notes on the efficacy of various kinds of treatment. Finally, the chemical nature of venoms has been analysed, they have been prepared in a pure state and their effects on laboratory animals have been studied in a way that could not be done with human victims. The result is that, in nearly every case, venomous animals have been found to present far less of a danger than is popularly believed.

In a few instances, it has been impossible to find an authentic record of fatality from an animal reputedly lethal. The exaggeration of the threat posed by an animal may be put into perspective by examining the common European viper or adder. The mere appearance of this snake is likely to elicit an attack with sticks, boots and anything else which comes to hand. Fear of the adder has led to harmless grass snakes, smooth snakes and slow-worms (which are legless lizards, not snakes) becoming tarred with the same brush and slaughtered indiscriminately. Yet the adder's bite is rarely more severe than a wasp sting and only seven fatalities were recorded in England and Wales during the first half of this century, and four of these were children. Moreover, when approached, the adder is most likely to slip away quietly; it will only attack when cornered and provoked.

This is an important point. In attacking, an animal can kill or maim its adversary but it may get killed itself. It is far safer to retreat. For this reason venomous animals are usually noticed only when they are forced to fight and have been unable to slip away unseen. Therefore, they get the reputation of attacking on sight. The situation can be summed up by saying: 'This animal is very bad; when it is attacked, it defends itself.'

Another point to be remembered is that the bite or sting is not 100 per cent efficient. Western films give a false impression when the hero's shots kill cleanly every time. The revolver is not an accurate weapon. Similarly, snakes may strike and miss, and accounts of snakebite usually omit the number of bites which have resulted in little or no venom being injected.

The words 'venom' and 'poison' are almost synonymous but venom is usually used to describe a poison which is injected by stinging or biting. Thus, snakes, scorpions, spiders and wasps are venomous, while toads, pufferfishes and blister beetles are poisonous. They have to be eaten to be harmful.

All spiders are venomous. They are predators, feeding on the tissues of other animals, which must first be subdued or killed. Poison is injected by means of a pair of hollow fangs, so that a spider can be said to stab rather than sting or bite. Its mouthparts are designed for sucking up the juices of its prey; it cannot chew solid food and the victim is eventually discarded as a dry husk. The spider's fangs are like the teeth of a lion or the fangs of a snake. Their primary use is to secure food but they also have a defensive function. If the predator is itself in danger, it can turn its weapons on its attacker.

Spiders are a good illustration of the bad name which venomous animals attract. Although all species bear venomous fangs, very few are dangerous to Man. The majority cannot penetrate human skin with their fangs but their appearance produces an irrational fear in many people (including the author) which is not based on their capacity to harm. It seems to be based on their overall physical appearance; the long legs, the gross swollen abdomen and, very often, the coat of coarse hair. Why fear should be induced in some people, who may be quite happy to hold a snake, while others will let a spider crawl over them but be terrified of a fluttering bird, is a matter for psychologists to explain. Even the giant bird-eating spider *below left* which really can eat birds, is a rather inoffensive animal. The main hazard from handling it is irritation from the hairs, and it may just threaten its foes by raising its forelegs like the baboon spider *right*. This spider lives in burrows. If a stick is pushed down the burrow, the spider rushes up it and onto your arm, giving quite a shock if nothing else.

The European crab spider *top left* can change its colour to match its background and is frequently encountered sitting in flowers mimicking the yellow stamens. When an unsuspecting insect visits the flower, the spider pounces on it. Hoverflies and other flower-loving flies are its chief prey, but butterflies and even bumblebees larger than the spider itself are caught and quickly subdued by its venomous bite.

It is unfortunate that spiders should have such a poor reputation because they do no harm in the main and, as insect eaters, they play an important part in wildlife economy. Their habits also make them one of the most interesting groups of animals to study. Although related, spiders are not insects. They are distinguished by their four pairs of legs and two-part bodies.

As exclusive predators, the spiders have invented a number of cunning stratagems for catching their food. Many are active hunters, like the wolf spiders and the bird-eating spiders. They are swift runners and have large eyes so they can seek out and run down their prey. The name tarantula *bottom left* is usually given to any big hairy spider but the true tarantula is a wolf spider native to southern Europe. From Roman times onwards, it was held that the bite of a tarantula induced a fatal melancholia and that the only cure was to dance furiously until all symptoms had disappeared. The dance was infectious and whole villages would join in, impelled by a mass hysteria. In later times, the dance became more sedate and had specially composed music–the tarantella.

The jumping spiders leap on their prey from a distance and, should they miss and fall, they are saved by the thread of silk that trails back to the point of take-off. Crab spiders, like the one eating a butterfly *bottom right*, lurk in flowers for insects seeking nectar and pollen. The spiders are so well matched with their background that they are very difficult to see even by the human eye which is much more sensitive than that of an insect.

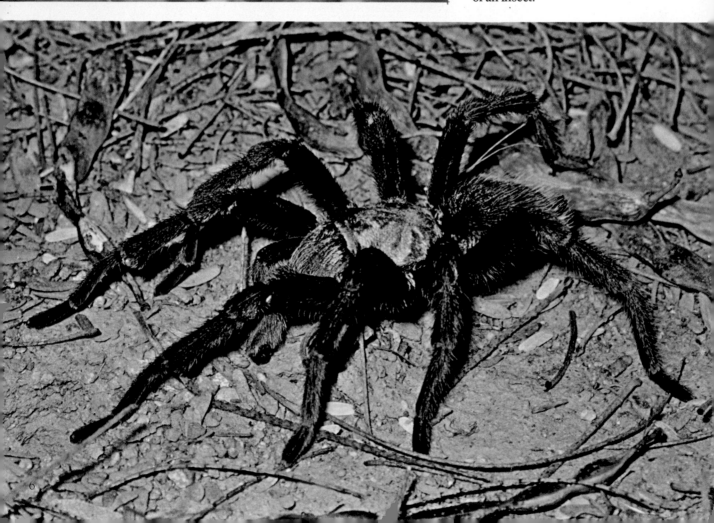

Everyone is familiar with the orb webs *top left* and cobwebs of spiders. The silken frame is used as a net to intercept flying insects and is provided with sticky threads or blobs of gum to hold the victim until the spider, alerted by its struggles, can rush out and seize it. There are many variations on this theme. The trapdoor spiders live in a silk-lined tunnel in the soil which is closed by a tightly-fitting, camouflaged lid. Silk trip wires radiate from the tube so that the spider knows the instant that some small animal wanders into range. The purse spiders spin a tube that lies on the ground and connects with a tunnel. When an insect walks over the tube, the spider seizes it with its fangs, cuts a slit in the silk and hauls the victim in.

A stranger stratagem is used by the net-casting spider *top right* whose web works on the butterfly net principle. The web is stretched between the spider's legs and is used to sweep up passing insects. The strangest trick of all is used by certain spiders which have no web but spin a single thread with a sticky blob at the end. This is whirled until it 'hooks' an insect.

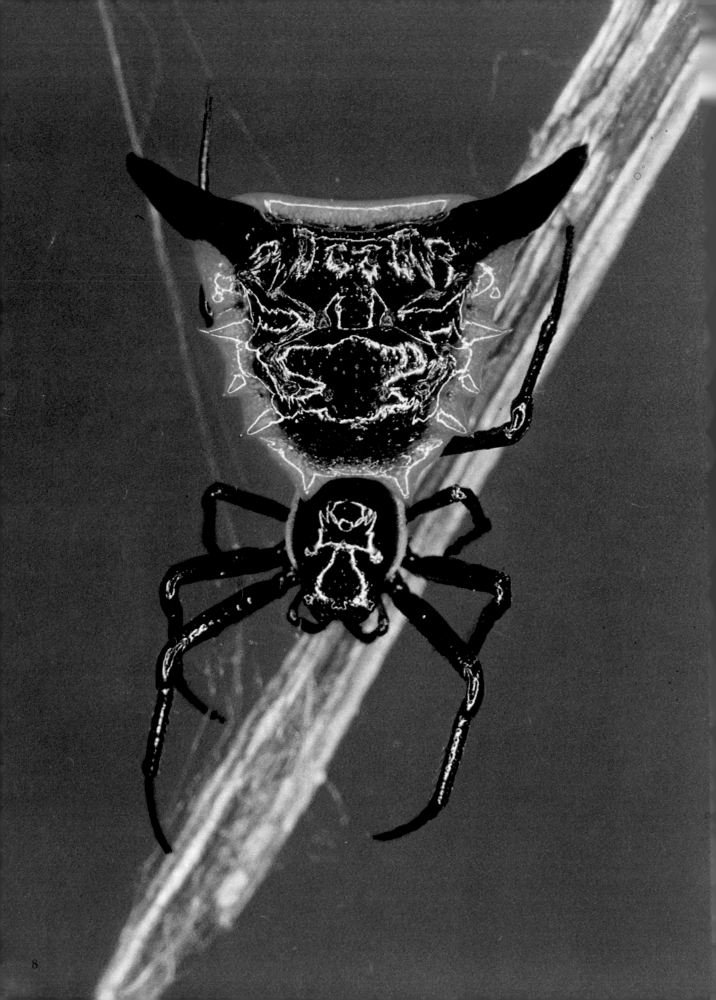

The thorn spider *left* is a South American species, but similar spiny-bodied spiders are found throughout the tropics. They are usually small, but conspicuous because of their bright, warning colours, usually black with red and yellow. They are not known to be poisonous to man, but are probably very distasteful to birds and other snappers-up of small invertebrates.

Perhaps the most dangerous of all spiders is the black widow *top right*. It appears innocuous–only ½ inch long, with a shiny black body and no hairs. On the underside there is a red mark in the perfect shape of an hour-glass, which has earned the species the alternative names of hour-glass spider and red mark. Black widows are found in many of the warmer parts of North America and near relatives include the redback of Australia, the katipo of New Zealand and the malmignatte of Mediterranean Europe. As the black widow's venom is said to be 15 times more powerful than that of a rattlesnake, it is an animal to be treated with caution. In fact, the black widow is shy and retiring.

The danger from a black widow comes from its habit of rushing out to investigate anything that vibrates its web and attacking whether it is a fly or a human finger. The web is built across a gap, where insects are likely to fly. In the days of primitive sanitation, the outdoor privy made a good place for a web with the result that most attacks have been on particularly tender parts. In 1,291 known cases of bites recorded in the United States during the 200 years prior to 1943, only 55 resulted in death. Shock, particularly to young or elderly people, is the main cause of death in many instances.

The symptoms of spider bite are unpleasant. The venom is a neurotoxin which causes paralysis, muscular cramp and severe pain. Breathing becomes difficult and the victim runs a high fever.

Most spiders are not harmful to man, but some large species have fangs long and strong enough to penetrate human skin. One such is the baboon spider of Africa *middle right and page 5*. But its bite, although painful, has an effect less than that of a wasp sting. Here the spider is seen in a beneficial role eating army worms, the very destructive moth caterpillar that devours grass as locusts devour leaves.

The Brazilian huntsman spider *bottom right* is another large species capable of delivering a venomous bite. Like other wolf spiders it captures its prey by running it down. Eyesight is therefore more important to this agile, active creature than it is to web-spinners that only sit and wait.

The soft, fleshy body of a caterpillar is a tempting morsel for any bird but some caterpillars are disagreeable. The stinging nettle caterpillar *top left* bears a bristling array of spines which burn and irritate the skin of anyone who handles it. Some American caterpillars cause severe pain, vomiting and fainting.

The caterpillars of the tiger moth and cinnabar moth *top right and far right* have a different strategy. Instead of poisonous spines or stings, their bodies contain alkaloids; substances which are unpleasant in small doses and very harmful in quantity. The poison does not save a particular caterpillar from being eaten but a bird learns that, in future, it is wise to leave well alone all caterpillars with bright yellow or orange markings. The caterpillar is sacrificed so that its kindred may live.

A millipede *bottom right* is distinguished from a centipede *bottom left* by the two pairs of legs to each body segment. Centipedes are fast running carnivores and have a bite which can be very serious. Millipedes, by contrast, are slow-moving vegetarians. They protect themselves by means of stink glands along the sides of the body. Some millipedes secrete hydrocyanic acid; others benzoquinone.

Like the bright colours of the caterpillars on the previous page, the bold patterning on the body of a ladybird *top left* shows that it is distasteful. When handled, ladybirds squirt blood from the joints of their legs. The blood of insects is not contained within blood vessels but floods through the body, bathing the tissues. When alarmed, the ladybird raises its blood pressure by compressing the abdomen, and the thin cuticle of the leg joints ruptures. A close relative is the bloody-nosed beetle which secretes blood from its mouth.

One effect of the beetle's blood is to clog the jaws of other insects attacking it. This could be happening to the wood ants attacking the ladybird *below left*. Wood ants do not sting, as do other ants. They bite with their powerful jaws then pour formic acid from the tip of the abdomen into the wound. If a wood ant nest is disturbed, the ants respond by squirting formic acid into the air. Stirring the nest, which is a pile of plant fragments, with a stick results in an overpowering reek of formic acid. Apart from deterring intruders, the acid acts as a signal to alert other ants. When one ant squirts acid, the vapour diffuses through the air and all ants within a radius of a few inches run about with jaws open. They, too, squirt acid. When the disturbance abates, the ants stop spraying, the formic acid disperses and the nest settles down. But if the disturbance continues, yet more ants are alerted and go on the defensive, so that formic acid squirting is an alarm that gears the size of the defence effort to the degree of disturbance.

One of the largest spiders in the world is the bird-eating spider *right*, an inhabitant of the Amazon jungle. By day it hides away in rock crevices, under loose bark or in a hollow tree, where it rests on a cosy pad of silk. At night it creeps stealthily out to forage. It spins no web but runs down its prey or seizes it in a silent pounce. A powerful creature, it is able to tackle a small mouse or drag a hummingbird from its nest. As soon as such prey is seized it is stabbed by the spider's sharp hollow fangs and injected with a quickly-lethal dose of venom.

The most frequent cause of stings are the bees, wasps and ants, of the insect order Hymenoptera. These are the social insects which often live in vast colonies. Most of the inhabitants of a nest are workers, which do not breed but spend their lives gathering food and tending the eggs and larvae of the queen bee, wasp or ant. The workers are sterile females and their egg-laying apparatus has been transformed into a sting which delivers a powerful venom. The shaft of the sting is a modified ovipositor or egg-laying tube. It consists of two lancets which slide to and fro in a sheath, to drill into the victim's skin. Venom is then pumped into the wound. A bee's sting is barbed and cannot be withdrawn from the tough skin of a large animal. It is torn from the body of the bee, which soon dies.

Insect venom is a complex mixture of pain-causing substances. That of wasps *top left and right* contains histamine, a substance which occurs naturally in the human body. Injection into the skin results in a 'nettle-rash'–redness, blistering and itching–while larger doses cause difficulty with breathing. Another component of wasp venom is hyaluronidase, an enzyme which dissolves the cement which binds tissue cells together, thereby allowing the venom to spread. Other pain inducers include 5-hydroxytryptamine and kinins. Hornet venom *bottom left* contains similar components. Wasp and hornet venoms do not contain strong alkalis; neither does bee venom contain acid. So traditional remedies of applying dilute ammonia to neutralise acid or vinegar to counteract alkali are ineffective. Cold compresses and soothing lotions alleviate mild stings but severe stings may require medical attention and the injection of antihistamines, epinephrine or calcium lactate. Reaction to venom varies from individual to individual. Some people are extremely sensitive and can suffer severely or even die from a single sting. Anyone known to be susceptible to insect venom can be desensitised by a course of treatment which involves giving the patient gradually increasing doses so that the body can build up its defences.

Among the largest wasps is this African spider-hunting wasp *below*. The female digs a burrow in which to lay her egg. She then seeks out a baboon spider and after a lengthy skirmish paralyses it with her sting, then drags it underground and lays an egg on it. When her larva hatches it feeds on the tissues of the inert spider which, one hopes, is anaesthetised as well as paralysed.

The brilliant yellow African crab spider *following page* is the same species as the pink-and-white individual among pink-and-white flowers (*page* 7). This one will not try to match the purple of the iris petals over which it is now hurrying, but will settle again in the flower's yellow centre, perfectly camouflaged.

The assassin bugs *right, top and bottom*, also called kissing bugs and masked hunters, are predatory insects which, like all true bugs, feed by sucking juices. They are named for the speed with which they seize their victims. They clasp them with powerful forelegs which fold like jack-knives. Once secure, the victim is killed by a powerful toxic saliva injected into its body through the bug's tubular beak. The saliva not only attacks the victim's nerves and muscles, causing paralysis, it also breaks down the body tissues which are sucked into the bug's stomach. The power of the saliva allows an assassin bug no more than a half inch long to overcome cockroaches, many times its size, in a matter of seconds and one large assassin bug attacks the giant rhinoceros beetle of Africa. The beetle is heavily armoured but its 'Achilles heel' is the cuticle at the joints of its legs which is soft enough for the bug's beak to penetrate.

Insects are the main prey of assassin bugs but some tropical species attack reptiles, birds and mammals and suck their blood. One species descends into bedrooms from crevices in the ceiling at night to attack the sleeping occupants. Another has a stab which is said to feel like an electric shock. Worse than the pain of the stab is the transmission of Chagas' disease by the large black benchuca of South America. Chagas' disease is caused by a protozoan parasite which lives in the blood. The disease is spread by the parasites being carried by the bug from an infected person and injected into the new victim's bloodstream. Charles Darwin has recorded his disgust at benchucas crawling over his body at night and the incurable mystery disease from which he suffered in later life was probably Chagas' disease.

A West Indian assassin bug secretes a fluid which is very attractive to ants. It intoxicates them and they fall an easy prey to the bug. Another large assassin bug uses its saliva to deter predators. It squirts its saliva over distances of one foot, with considerable accuracy. And by rotating its head with the beak in the folded position it can shoot over its back. Scientists studying this assassin bug report that a jet of saliva in the eye causes temporary blindness.

Toads are protected from their enemies by a venom contained in two glands behind the eyes, the parotid glands. The venom contains a number of substances called variously bufotenins, bufotalins and bufagins. Some have the same effect as the drug digitalis. They cause the heartbeat to slow down and the blood pressure to rise, with accompanying nausea and swelling. Before digitalis was extracted from foxgloves, dried and powdered toad skin was used to cure dropsy and, centuries ago, the Chinese used toad venom to stop gum bleeding and to cure toothache.

The giant marine toad *above left*, which has no particular affinities with the sea, has been spread from its native tropical America to most of the warmer parts of the world. It is a pest because it eats large numbers of native animals, while predators are killed by its poison, or from its habit of blowing up its body so that it becomes stuck in its devourer's gullet.

The African common toad *bottom left* squats at a pond's edge advertising its presence to potential mate or rival males by pumping out loud croaks amplified by his inflated vocal sac. He is generally unmolested by predators on account of his venom glands, although the very many kinds of frogs which share the same habitat, but are not similarly protected, fall prey to herons, storks, kingfishers and other water birds, as well as to otters, mongooses and all sorts of other predators.

The attractive red and black frog *right* is the two-toned arrow poison frog of South America. With many of its relatives it is one of the most poisonous animals. Predators recognise that the bright colours are a warning of the frog's toxicity.

Although living inoffensively in trees or on the ground, where they hunt small insects, arrow poison frogs are famous for their use by South American Indians who use the venom on the tips of their arrows. The Indians collect the poison by impaling the frog on a sharp stick and holding it over a fire. The heat causes the poison fluid to exude from glands in the skin and collect in droplets which can be scraped off. Called batrachotoxin, it is the most powerful animal venom known and is 250 times more toxic than strychnine.

The common European toad *above left, right* is a figure of horror for some and was the subject of folklore in ancient times. Its mere presence was said to pollute the ground. On the other hand, the toad was said to bear a stone in its head. When cut out, the touchstone was invaluable because it changed colour in the presence of poisoned food and drink. It also cured snakebite.

In reality, the toad secretes poison from the glands on its head. If a dog takes a toad into its mouth, it quickly drops it and starts to salivate copiously.

Bright colours, like those of the painted reed frog *left, bottom* often mean that the owner is poisonous. In some settings, the pattern of wavy lines could be a camouflage but, when sitting on a waterlily, it is likely to be advertising itself. Cattle are said to have been killed by these frogs, after eating them while grazing.

Hydra *left, above and below* is a voracious inhabitant of ponds and ditches. It is a relative of the anemones of the seashore. Its body is a hollow tube fixed to a water plant at one end and having a mouth surrounded by a ring of tentacles at the other. Both these hydras are reproducing by budding off a new individual from the side of the body. Eventually the new hydra will break free and lead an independent life.

Hydras feed on small animals–the one in the top picture has caught a kind of water flea. If an animal blunders into the trailing tentacles, it is immediately seized, conveyed to the mouth and bundled in. When the prey's tissues have been digested, its shell or skeleton is ejected. To help capture the prey, the tentacles are armed with hundreds of minute stinging cells, or nematocysts. Each nematocyst consists of a sac containing a hollow, coiled-up thread. On triggering by touch or chemical stimulus from the victim's body, the lid of the nematocyst flies open and the thread shoots out with such force that it penetrates the victim's body. Barbs help to hold it fast and poison is pumped down the thread to stop its struggles. Hydras are about one centimetre long and are no danger to large animals.

The well-named porcupinefish or horned puffer is a very dangerous animal. The danger lies not in its spines but in its flesh. Pufferfishes are also called globefishes, blowfishes or swellfishes because of their habit of inflating themselves when molested. If that was not sufficient defence, many parts of the body contain the poison tetrodotoxin. Without any means of biting or stinging, puffers would not seem to be a danger to the human race if it were not for the fact that puffers are considered a delicacy. Puffers live in most of the warmer seas of the world and they are eaten in the Far East, particularly in Japan where they are called *fugu*. The poison is concentrated in the skin, reproductive organs, liver and intestines, and extreme care is needed in the preparation of the flesh before it can be cooked.

About 50 people are poisoned by puffers every year in Japan, and over half die. The poison acts quickly. Within half an hour, the victim is feeling weak and dizzy with tingling around the throat and mouth. Tingling and numbness spread and sweating, difficulty in breathing and bleeding ensue. Finally there is paralysis and perhaps death.

There is a Japanese saying: Great is the temptation to eat fugu but greater is the dread of dying.

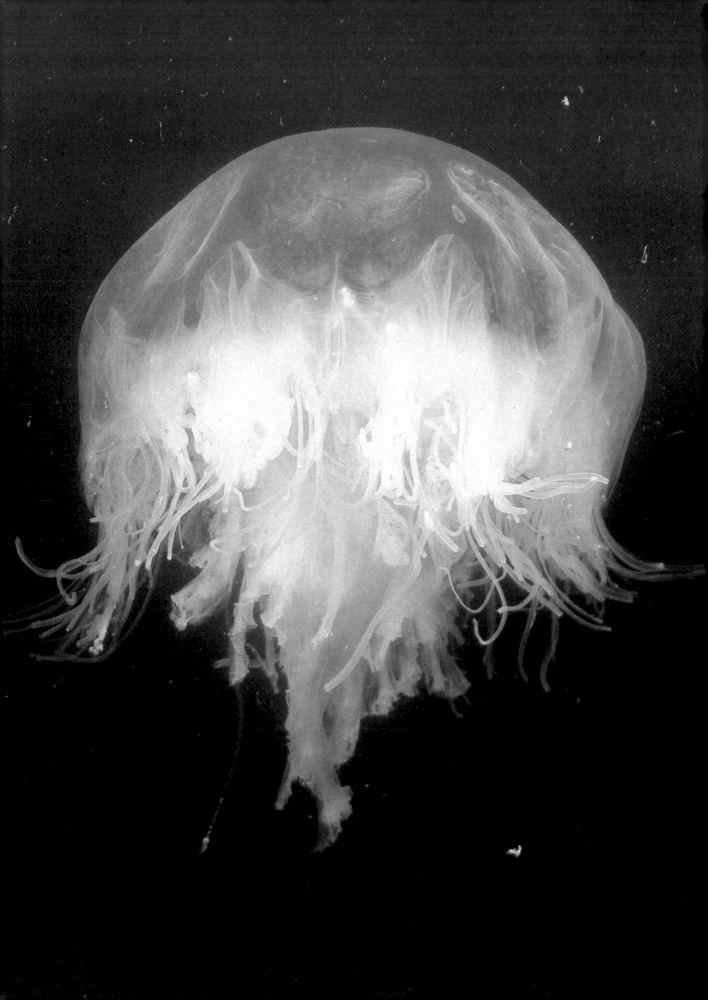

Left and right top the violet jellyfish. Jellyfish float through the sea, at the whim of current and wind. Each is equipped with an array of tentacles studded with nematocysts or stinging cells. Small animals, fishes, shrimps and the like, blunder into the tentacles, are stung by the nematocysts and swept into the mouth on the underside of the body. Most jellyfish are harmless to human beings but a few, living in the tropics, are dangerous, even fatal. After the body has touched the tentacles of a dangerous species, burning pain is instantaneous. Weals and blisters follow with, in severe cases, difficult breathing and mental confusion. Death can occur in a few minutes.

The Portuguese Man o' War *right, below* is not a true jellyfish. Each individual is, in fact, a colony of many individual organisms. It is buoyed by a gas-filled float by which it is blown by the wind over the surface of the sea. Dangling from the float there are a number of long tentacles which are used for catching fish. Portuguese Men o' War are found mainly in the tropics but they may be blown into temperate waters. The sting is very painful and is occasionally fatal.

The common freshwater pufferfish *top left* of Southeast Asia lives in brackish water and swamps. It is often imported as an aquarium fish and is unusual in lacking the spines of other pufferfishes. Its complicated patterning of rings and curves gives it camouflage as it rests motionless among water plants. But if it is disturbed, the same markings are eye-catching and act as a warning not to touch it. It can give a painful nip with its mouth and any animal that eats it will suffer from its poisonous flesh.

The cuttlefish *left middle*, octopus and squid are marine relatives of slugs and snails. In appearance there is little resemblance between the crawling, plant-eating slugs and snails and the fast-moving sea creatures, which are carnivorous. Fishes and shrimps are caught with the tentacles with incredible rapidity. It takes only 3/100 of a second to whip out the tentacles and draw in the victim. It is pulled towards the mouth where it is seized with a horny, parrot-like beak. There, the victim is immobilised with a venomous saliva. Although cuttlefish grow up to five feet, including the tentacles, they are usually much smaller and are no danger to human beings.

Barracuda *left bottom* are feared for their sharp teeth. They are fast-swimming fish which strike with great force to cause severe wounds, including amputation of limbs. However, like sharks, barracuda are unpredictable and attacks on human beings are luckily rare. More dangerous is the poisonous nature of barracuda flesh. Barracuda are eaten in many parts of the world and they sometimes cause cases of *ciguatera*. This is a general name for poisoning by eating certain fish, particularly barracuda, groupers, snappers and basses and others which live around coral reefs. The poison is concentrated mainly in the liver, skin and reproductive organs and is thought to originate from the fish eating poisonous algae or, in the case of carnivores like barracuda, eating fish already containing the poison. The poison attacks the nerves and can be fatal.

Danger lurks in the body of the beautiful and bizarre dragonfish *right*. Also called zebrafish or lionfish, eighteen of its many spines carry venom. A sting is excruciatingly painful for several hours but most victims recover. When disturbed, the dragonfish turns to present its venomous spines.

The slug-like sea cucumber *left, top* is a relative of the starfishes and sea urchins. When disturbed it secretes venom through the skin or ejects poisonous threads through the back passage. The venom causes vomiting and people in Guam catch fish by squeezing the body fluids of sea cucumbers into rock pools.

The sea hare *left, bottom* is a bizarre relative of the seashore periwinkle. It gets its name from two flaps of skin which resemble the ears of a hare. The Romans and Greeks credited it with almost satanic powers but it is inoffensive. However, although it is a vegetarian, its digestive juices contain a poison which can kill small animals.

The rhizostome jellyfish *right* of the Atlantic can give a nasty, burning sting. Fever and weakness may last for a day.

30

The pop-eyed squid of the Carribean *left* is more beautiful than its name suggests. The squid is a fast-moving relative of the cuttlefish. Squid of different sizes are found throughout the seas of the world and some grow to enormous sizes. The record length is 60 feet. Some squid are aggressive. They may attack and bite with their horny beaks but the poison of squid, and most octopuses, is not very potent.

In contrast, the stonefish *right, top* is one of the most dangerous marine animals. The three species live in the Indian and Pacific Oceans and frequent shallow water, where they are a great danger to bathers and people who make a living by fishing in shallow water. Part of the danger lies in the way that the stonefish lies on the seabed, looking like a stone or lump of coral, and is almost impossible to see. If accidentally trodden on, it lashes out with its poison spines. Almost immediately, the victim is writhing in agony. He may become delirious and have to be forcibly held down. Death may ensue within a few hours and if the victim survives, the agony lasts for 12 hours. Flesh around the wound sloughs off and a year elapses before recovery is complete.

Although not so lethal as a stonefish, stingrays cause more accidents. They are found all over the world, from the tropics to temperate seas. Most live in shallow water, along beaches and mudflats and a few come into brackish or fresh water, so it is easy to tread on them. Their habit is to lie on the seabed, hidden under a layer of sand or mud. The sting is in the tail. It is a long sharp spine, serrated along both edges and with a groove along its length to carry the venom.

When an unwary foot treads on a stingray, the tail whips up and the sting is thrust into the victim's leg. Poison aside, the sting causes a nasty wound and occasionally breaks off so that surgery is needed to remove it. Thousands of people suffer from stingrays every year but very few die. Most need the wound closed but few require much treatment for the venom. Its effects are largely local. The pain reaches its maximum intensity in about an hour and lasts up to two days. There may also be sickness, fainting and cramp. First aid consists of washing the wound to remove the venom and bathing in very hot water.

Scorpionfishes *left* are widely distributed, mainly in warm seas but many live in temperate waters. Like the stonefish, scorpionfishes are well camouflaged and easily overlooked so that there is a danger of treading on their poison spines. A more frequent cause of stings comes from scorpionfishes being caught by anglers and fishermen. There are several hundred cases reported each year in the United States alone, arising from anglers being stung while removing scorpionfishes from the hook or while cleaning the fishes. Housewives are also stung by fish brought home for the pot. Luckily, the venom is not too potent but the pain can be severe for hours, while swelling and tenderness last for several days.

Pufferfishes, or globefishes *right top* are closely related to the porcupinefish shown on page 23. The picture shows one fish in the normal shape and one that has blown itself up with air or water to escape being eaten. An eight inch puffer takes in a quart of water. At the same time, the spines are raised to make the puffer a floating pincushion. The poison is mainly concentrated in the skin, liver and reproductive organs. So any predator not put off by the ballon-shaped body and spines dies a painful death. At one time the Polynesian islanders used puffer poison on the tips of their spears. They call puffers *maki-maki* meaning deadly death.

The parrotfishes *right bottom* are named after the way their teeth are joined to make a 'parrot's beak' in the front of the mouth. The beak is used to crunch up lumps of coral. Like many other fishes living around coral reefs, parrotfishes can cause ciguatera poisoning when they are eaten (see Barracuda page 26).

Sea anemones *left* are related to jelly-fish and the freshwater hydra and have the same stinging cells or nematocysts in their tentacles for catching their prey. Some sea anemones have nematocysts powerful enough to penetrate human skin. One sea anemone causes 'sponge fisherman's disease'. This consists of itching and burning, followed by ulceration, fever and vomiting. It is sometimes fatal. Very rarely bathers accidentally swallow broken tentacles with very unpleasant results, even death.

Sea urchins *right* are globe-shaped animals best known for their hollow shells which are thrown on the beach after storms. In life, the body is covered with a thick pile of spines and pincer-like organs called pedicellariae, as well as the tube feet on which the sea urchin walks. The spines are used for walking, digging into sand, feeding and for protection. Some sea urchins have spines which carry a venom. When touched, the spines penetrate the skin and break off. The venom causes a sharp pain and inflammation and secondary infections may occur. The spine, itself, is eventually dissolved in the body and surgery is not needed to remove it. The pedicellariae also grip offending bodies and venom stored in their jaws is injected.

The delicately branching hydroids *left top* are aptly called sea firs in Britain and sea plumes in the United States. They could be easily mistaken for plants as they poise motionless in the water but a powerful hand lens would reveal that the 'leaves' are minute animals, called polyps, each one with a slender body and a ring of tentacles like a miniature sea anemone. Sea firs are called 'colonial animals' because the polyps are connected through the 'twigs'. Sea firs feed on minute crustaceans and worms, even on tiny fishes.

The sea anemones *right* take larger prey. Any animal which brushes against the tentacles is immediately seized by the nematocysts and slowly poisoned, so that, helpless, it is stuffed into the anemone's mouth. Once inside the bag-like stomach, digestive juices set to work and the victim is reduced to a skeleton.

A similar fate seems to be falling to the clown anemonefish or orange anemonefish *left bottom* but this fish is immune to the stings of nematocysts. It is protected by a covering of mucus or slime which contains a substance that inhibits the sea anemone's nematocysts. If the mucus is washed off, the anemonefish is immediately stung and killed. It used to be thought that, in return for giving protection, the anemone received some of the fish's food. Anemonefish do take food back to the anemone but eat it themselves. If a morsel is dropped, a tug-of-war ensues and the fish tears it away before it reaches the anemone's mouth.

The brilliant red of the cardinal beetle *top left* advertises its bad taste. Birds learn that bright red insects are unpleasant to eat. The result is that cardinal beetles can crawl over flowers without fear. They are very common on herbaceous plants of country lanes. Other insects fly away when disturbed but cardinal beetles take no notice; they rely on their warning coloration to give them immunity.

The blister beetles *bottom left* are distasteful relatives of the cardinal beetle. Blister beetles are so named because their blood contains cantharidin, a poison which raises blisters and causes a burning sensation. The most famous blister beetle is the Spanish Fly, which has been used as an aphrodisiac sometimes with dire results. Cantharidin has been used with greater benefit in the treatment of bladder disorders.

Biting flies, like mosquitoes and tsetse flies, are a scourge because of the many terrible diseases they transmit; the bites alone however can cause great misery if one is plagued by flies. The horsefly *right* transmits no disease but can give a nasty bite. 'Bite' is perhaps not the correct word. The mouthparts are like a hypodermic needle and they stab the flesh so the fly can suck up a meal of blood. The pain comes from anticoagulant saliva which is pumped into the wound.

Ants are a danger because of their mass-action. Although an individual ant is a small, insignificant animal, it lives in colonies of tens of thousands. When aroused in defence, swarms of ants muster to attack and deliver a heavy blow to the enemy. Most ants seize an enemy with their jaws to get a good purchase before stinging and the venom may enter through the wound of the bite. Wood ants *right, middle* spray enemies with a 50 per cent solution of formic acid. The spray kills soft-bodied insects on contact and others die as the spray penetrates their breathing organs. Driver ants *top right* are nomads. The entire colony, including queen, eggs and larvae, moves in a vast swarm over the countryside, devouring any animal that gets in their way. Tethered horses and livestock are reduced to skeletons if they cannot break free. The damage is done with the huge jaws of the ants which lack a sting. To protect themselves they either use their jaws or squirt a fluid with repellant and insecticidal properties.

Bulldog ants *top left and far left and overleaf* live in Australia where the large mounds which comprise their nests are places to be avoided. Vibration from approaching footsteps, or even a shadow falling over the nest, provokes a stream of angry worker ants to pour out. The jaws, built like a pair of coal tongs are awesome enough, but the main armament of the bulldog ant is its sting. The worker ants are one inch long and they seize the flesh of an unwary intruder with a tenacity which earns their name of bulldog.Then the body curls forward and the long sting delivers its venom. One sting sends waves of pain coursing through the body and lasts for several days. As few as 30 stings can kill a man.

The food of bulldog ants is insects which they kill with a sting before sucking their juices or carrying them back to feed to their larvae. The harvester ants *bottom left and right* are mainly plant eaters and carry seeds back to the nest but some of the workers have extra large heads and jaws *right*. These are the soldiers which guard the other workers and attack other insects.

Scorpions *right and overleaf* are eight-legged relatives of the spiders. They live in warm countries and are particularly abundant in dry, desert regions. One kind lives in the European Alps. The pair of pincers, the pedipalps, are harmless and are used for tearing up food but the curved sting in the tip of the tail is to be avoided. There are more cases of scorpion sting than snakebite in the United States, for instance, where the two lethal species caused 64 deaths in a 20 year period.

Scorpions range in length from ¼ in. to over 8 inches but size is not a criterion for deadliness. As a general rule, smaller scorpions are more deadly than larger species. The giant lobster-scorpion of Sumatra has never been convicted of stinging a human being, because it is shy and lives deep in forests. The two lethal American species are 2-3 inches long and, like many species, they are a hazard because they come into houses. Scorpions are active at night and hide away in crevices by day. The result is that they can turn up in shoes, piles of clothing, bedding and in furniture. An incautious foot or hand thrust into boot or shirt is a sitting target. With any luck, a scorpion will give warning of its intent to attack by giving a warning sound. This is made by the rasping of the mouthparts against the roof of the mouth, the legs rubbing together or the tip of the tail rubbing on the abdomen. The attack is delivered by the tail whipping forward. The curved sting is connected to two large venom glands which pump a neurotoxin into the victim. The venom is more powerful than that of some of the most deadly snakes. The symptoms are like those of strychnine poisoning. Apart from the pain, there is vomiting, sweating, shivering and difficulty of speech. Froth comes out of the mouth and nose and finally there are convulsions before death intervenes.

There is a story that, if a scorpion is placed inside a ring of fire, it will commit suicide by stinging itself. The truth of the matter is more likely to be that the heat from the fire causes the tail to bend over and give the impression of a self-inflicted sting.

Only two kinds of mammal are known to be venomous. The shrews are small, restless, mouse-like animals, rarely seen except as corpses on country paths. Their main food is insects but they also attack larger animals. Water shrews *left above and below* can kill frogs bigger than themselves. They have special salivary glands which open at the base of the lower incisor teeth. The glands produce a neurotoxin which causes paralysis and death in small animals. Venom from American short-tailed shrews has been injected in mice. It causes death within a few minutes. Shrews are only likely to bite human beings when handled but the venom causes reddening of the skin and a burning pain which lasts for a few days.

The duck-billed platypus *above and right* is one of the two monotremes which live in Australia. The monotremes are strange mammals with many peculiarities, including laying eggs rather than giving birth to live young. Platypuses live in burrows in river banks and feed on small water animals such as insects, snails and crustaceans. The male platypus bears a curved, hollow spur on the inside of each ankle. The spur is connected to poison glands in the thigh and venom is secreted during the breeding season. The use of the poison spurs is not known. If they were used during male rivalry in the breeding season, it would seem that they could be better placed on the body.

Attacks on human beings are very rare. A sting causes local swelling and pain and can be quite serious. One victim received both spurs in the hand, became seriously ill for weeks and lost the use of his arm.

The second monotreme, the spiny anteater or echidna, looks like a hedgehog or porcupine. It bears spurs but no one knows their purpose.

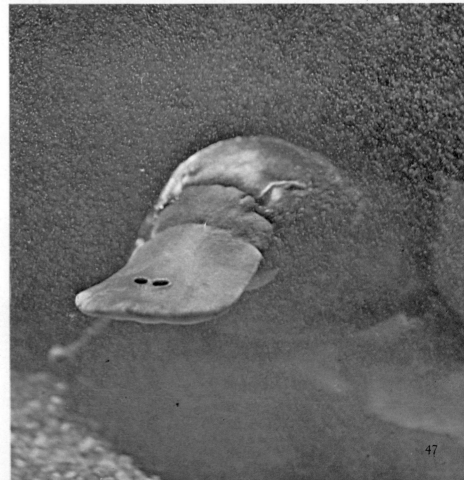

It is impossible to say which is the most dangerous of the world's snakes. So much depends on whether the snake frequents human habitation, whether it is common or rare, aggressive or shy. There are also differences in toxicity of the venom and the amount injected in a bite. The result is that experts differ in their assessment of the danger from snakebites. There is no way in which a poisonous snake can be distinguished from a harmless species, with the result that many harmless snakes lose their lives to people who are taking no chances. The situation is complicated by certain harmless snakes mimicking the appearance of venomous species so as to gain the same immunity from predators.

Snakes can be classed on the structure of their fangs. Non-venomous snakes, such as the grass snake, have no fangs and are called *aglyphs.* The back-fanged snakes, or *opisthoglyphs,* have fangs at the back of the mouth. Each fang has a groove down which venom flows. The African boomslang *right bottom* attacking a chameleon, is an opisthoglyph. To inject a good dose of venom, it hangs on to its victim and chews its flesh. If such a snake is struck away from the body immediately it has bitten, the bite will not be severe.

The cobras are *proteroglyphs* with fangs at the front of the mouth. The fangs of some proteroglyphs bear grooves while, in others, the sides of the grooves meet to form a canal. The Indian cobra *right top and middle* is a proteroglyph and is recognised by the hood which it inflates when excited. Indian cobras are one of the most dangerous snakes, killing, it has been estimated, 10,000 people a year in India. The mongoose is the traditional enemy of the cobra, being protected by its speed and immunity to snake venom.

The position of the fangs and the canal makes injection of venom more efficient but the most advanced biting apparatus belongs to the *solenoglyphs.* The vipers, the rattlesnakes, fer de lance and others have very long fangs, each served with a canal, which, when not in use, are folded along the roof of the mouth. The strike is rapid, the fangs being thrown forwards, and the snake then withdraws without chewing like the opisthoglyphs and proteroglyphs.

The mambas *left* are proteroglyphs with a very potent venom. The black mamba is notoriously aggressive. Proterglyph venom acts mainly on the nervous system, while that of solenoglyphs attacks the blood system and destroys tissues.

49

The sight of a snake evokes a quick reaction–to kill or to run away. Critical examination for identification could be dangerous. Two of these snakes are harmless; one is dangerous. The two North American king snakes, the scarlet *left* and the coral *below,* are harmless but they could be easily mistaken for venomous coral snakes. Unlike most snakes which are well camouflaged, coral snakes have bold bands of colour, and the king snakes are sometimes called 'false coral snakes' because they mimic the colouring of the coral snakes. They can, however, be told apart by the sequence of the bands, thus:

>Red on yellow (or white)
>Kill a fellow (or might)
>Red on black
>Venom lack.

The adder *right* is venomous and is recognised by the inverted V on the back of the head.

The fer de lance *top left* is a much feared snake of South and Central America and the West Indies. It grows to 6 ft and its habit of entering houses in search of rats and mice brings it into contact with Man.

The cottonmouth moccasin is a close relative of the fer de lance, and both are linked with rattlesnakes. The cottonmouth *below* is the third most dangerous snake in North America.

The spitting cobra *right* of Africa has fangs modified for squirting a jet of venom. The aperture is directed forwards and the spitting cobra can hit a target over 6 ft distant. It aims at the eyes and the venom causes intense pain and inflammation.

The rattlesnakes *right, top and bottom* are the most feared snakes in North America. They are named for the rattle on the tail *see right, bottom*. When disturbed, a rattlesnake will vibrate its tail causing the rattle to make a buzz audible over a distance of a few feet. The rattle is made up of a number of loosely interlocking segments each of which was once a scale originally covering the tail. In other snakes this scale is shed, with the rest of the skin, at each moult. The rattlesnakes retain the scale and the rattle is gradually built up but it does not grow indefinitely. The end scales eventually wear off. Wild rattlers rarely have more than 14 scales and a rattle with 8 makes the most noise. There are over 30 species of rattlesnake and the danger posed by them varies from species to species. The eastern and western diamondback rattlesnakes are bad-tempered and will pursue an intruder but the red diamond rattlesnake will often stand rough handling without attacking.

The harmless African green tree snake *top left* is probably protected from predators by its close resemblance to the venomous green mamba *bottom left*. Both snakes are agile climbers, hunting birds, treefrogs and other arboreal animals in bushes and low trees. The harmless snake can be identified by its overlapping scales.

An important part of our knowledge of snakes is how to treat bites. The production of antivenins has greatly reduced fatalities from these but the use of each antivenin is restricted to a single species or a group of species and, as there may be adverse reactions, all must be used with discretion. There is still disagreement about first aid. It is essential that the patient should be kept calm and removed to hospital as soon as possible, preferably with the corpse of the snake for identification. Other procedures such as the use of a tourniquet, cutting the wound or sucking out the venom are now usually discouraged since it is realised that such measures can cause more damage than does the actual venom injected, particularly by less dangerous species such as the adder *top centre*. Of course no undue risk should ever be taken with such a large and dangerous snake as the African viper *centre right*. Such snakes should only be handled by experts. It is fairly safe to hold a snake by gripping it close behind the head but even such giant vipers are quite delicate creatures and rough handling can result in extensive bruising from which the snake may never recover.

The sidewinder *left* is a desert-dwelling rattlesnake which adopts an unusual mode of locomotion to travel over loose sand. Instead of the usual serpentine movement, with waves passing down the body, the sidewinder's movement is rather like that of a caterpillar tractor. The snake throws its body into curves and, at any moment, only two points of the body touch the ground. Points anterior are laid down ahead of the part on the ground while points posterior are raised, and the sidewinder leaves its characteristic parallel tracks in the sand.

Boomslangs *right top* are more characteristically found in trees. They perch, immobile and camouflaged by the green skin, and wait for birds, tree frogs, chameleons and other small animals. They also raid nests.

Pit vipers *right bottom* are named after the small pit in the face, midway between eye and nostril. The pits are very sensitive heat detectors and are sensitive to changes of as little as $0.002°$ Centigrade. This means that a pit viper can detect the warmth of a human hand a foot away. With a pit on each side of the head, the snake can pinpoint sources of heat or cold and so strike at prey in pitch darkness.

The African puff adder *left top* is a member of the viper family. It gets its name from the hissing that warns of its displeasure. Although slow to strike, its venom is plentiful and potent. Fifteen drops can be delivered in a bite, and only four are needed to kill a man. The puff adder here is seen swallowing a grass rat; only the tail is still visible.

The European adder *left, bottom* is shown here with a brood of babies. Like all members of the viper family, the eggs hatch inside the mother's body and the young are born alive.

The sea snakes *right* spend their lives at sea, feeding on fish. They live in the Indian and Pacific Oceans and are a danger when they are brought aboard in fishing nets.

Fire salamanders *left, top* are amphibians related to newts. They can be distinguished from lizards because they have the soft, clammy skin of amphibians rather than the dry, scaly skin of reptiles. As might be expected, the bright yellow stripes and blobs are a warning that fire salamanders should be left alone. There is no sting nor fangs but the fire salamander secretes a venom from pores in the skin, just behind the eyes. The venom is a milky fluid called salamandrin. It is very uncomfortable to get into the eyes and mouth, or into an open cut.

In mediaeval times it was thought that the fire salamander had a fatal bite. Another story was that fire salamanders were unharmed by fire and that asbestos was 'salamander wool.'

The gila (pronounced *heela*) monster *left,
bottom* and the beaded lizard *right top* are
the only venomous lizards. The gila
monster lives in the southwestern
United States and the beaded lizard lives
in western Mexico. Surprisingly, the gila
monster was kept as a pet in such
numbers that it is now rare in the wild.
Its venom is more potent, drop for drop,
than that of rattlesnakes. The venom
is secreted from glands in the lower jaw
which opens around the base of the
teeth. When the gila monster bites,
venom washes around the teeth and is
worked into the wound by chewing.
Luckily, this method of injection is in-
efficient and if the lizard can be removed
quickly, very little of the venom is trans-
mitted. However, the gila monster has
a vice-like bite and most of the fatalities
have been due to repeated bites or the
victim being drunk. Nevertheless, the
bite is very severe, with swelling, vomiting and fainting.

The crested newt is an amphibian which
spends most of its life on land, returning
to water only to breed. It is the largest
European newt and grows to 6 inches.
During the breeding season the male
develops a frilly crest along its back.
Like the toad and the fire salamander,
crested newts exude a poison secretion
from pores on the back. It is sufficiently
unpleasant to deter would-be predators.
The body of the Californian newt
contains the venom tetrodotoxin, the
same as found in pufferfishes. So powerful is this venom that 1/3000 oz can kill
7000 mice, yet Californian newts are not
affected by their own poison and can
survive an injection of tetrodotoxin
25,000 times greater than that needed
to kill a frog.

The African green tree snake *overleaf
left* resembles the dangerous green
mamba but is non-venomous. The
bumble-bee *overleaf right*, while looking
harmless, has a venomous sting. It uses
this weapon against enemies such as
badgers and skunks which dig up bees'
nests to get at the honey. Unlike the
familiar honey-bee the bumble-bee
does not die after it has used its sting
on such animals. This is because the
sting is smooth, not barbed, and can
therefore be withdrawn after stinging.

INDEX